MAKE YOUR OWN
Christmas
DECORATIONS

MAKE YOUR OWN
Christmas
DECORATIONS

Cath Kidston®

Photography by Claire Richardson

Quadrille
PUBLISHING

26

30

34

50

54

58

Unless otherwise stated, the copyright and other intellectual property rights in all designs and patterns in this book are owned by Cath Kidston Limited. For the purposes of this legal notice, any use of the designs other than for your own personal use, including resale, is prohibited.

Introduction

Each year one of the special opportunities Christmas brings is the fun of putting up the decorations. You can buy all manner of Christmas products nowadays – the choice is really endless – but I think it is especially rewarding to make some of your own.

I have designed twelve hanging ornaments that are made from easy-to-sew felt and can be simply stitched together by sewers of all ages. The gift pack that accompanies this book contains the essential materials required to make up the twelve different decorations. All you need to add is a basic sewing kit of needles and scissors, plus a small amount of toy stuffing that is widely available at haberdashers, department stores and online. Once you have used up the felt provided in the gift pack, you can still make the decorations again and again by choosing your own materials in your favourite colours.

As well as looking festive on the tree, these felt ornaments can be used in all sorts of ways. Try adding them to a parcel when wrapping a gift, or strung along a length of ribbon and draped as a garland or even box them up as a gift.

However you decide to use them, have fun.

Cath Kidston

Cutting the felt shapes

All twelve of these fun festive ornaments can be created from just eleven medium-sized sheets of coloured felt. To get all the pieces needed, you must do some creative economic placement of the paper templates. If you follow the cutting guides below for each of the different colours, you will easily be able to cut all the pieces from the felt included in the pack. It is best the trace all the templates onto the felt sheets in one go, as that way you

won't miss out any shapes. You can then either snip out each shape as you need it or cut all of them in one go – if you do this, it is best to place the different pieces of coloured felt required for each ornament together in one labelled plastic bag or envelope for safe keeping. If you use an air-erasable pen to trace around the shapes, then you will need to cut out the shapes within 24–48 hours of tracing round the templates as your guidelines will disappear!

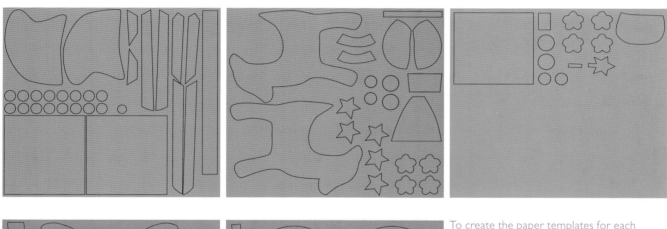

To create the paper templates for each decoration either photocopy the relevant pages at 100% or trace off the shapes onto paper. Carefully cut around each outline. The instructions for each decoration tell you how many of each shape are required and in which colour. Trace the larger shapes onto the felt first. Once the larger shapes are drawn, fill in the gaps with the smaller shapes, such as the red circles used for the berries on the Christmas Pudding, If you cut out the shapes following these guides, there will be a small amount of felt left over, which you can use to practice the basic embroidery stitches.

Working the basic stitches

You really don't have to be an expert sewer to make these Christmas decorations, you just need to be able to thread a needle and work basic straight edging stitches to join the different felt pieces together. Your stitching can be as perfectly neat or cheerfully haphazard as you can manage – I rather like the handmade look with visible stitches. Some of the decorations, such as the Frosty Snowman and Santa Claus use a specific stitch called a

Running Stitch

The most basic embroidery stitch, but also one of the most effective, especially when worked in a contrasting colour thread. Bring the needle up and back down through the fabric, working evenly sized and spaced small stitches in either a straight or shaped line. The stitches on the reverse side of the fabric should similarly be of equal length, but half the size or less than the stitches on the surface of the fabric.

Straight Edging Stitch

An easy stitch to master, when worked in matching embroidery thread, straight edging stitch gives a subtle finish when joining pieces of felt together. Larger stitches worked in a contrasting embroidery thread create a decorative effect. Work a round of evenly sized and spaced small stitches at right angles to the edge of the felt pieces.

French knot for embroidering the eyes. Instructions for how to work a French knot, along with three other basic stitches are given below. If you find any of the specific stitches too tricky, experiment by working any other stitch in its place. Whichever stitch you are working, you can vary the effect by using as many as the full six strands of the embroidery thread for visibly prominent stitches or a few as one or two strands for a more subtle finish.

Blanket Stitch

A great alternative to running stitch or straight edging stitches, blanket stitch is used to anchor appliqué pieces to a base fabric or to join two pieces of felt together. Start by bringing the needle up at A, take the needle back down at B and then up again, directly above, at C. Pull the needle through over the thread and repeat to the end.

French Knot

A stitch that requires a small amount of practice to perfect, this leaves a neat knot on the surface of a fabric. Bring the needle up at the position where the knot is required. Wrap the thread around the needle two or three times, then take the needle back down close to where the thread first emerged (although not in exactly the same place or the knot will simply pull back through).

Christmas Pudding

You will need

From the gift pack: Brown, cream, red and green felt • Brown, cream and red embroidery thread • Two red pompoms • 15cm length brown waxed cord

You will also need: Paper templates • Air-erasable pen • Sewing needle • Scissors • Polyester toy stuffing (see safety note on page 64)

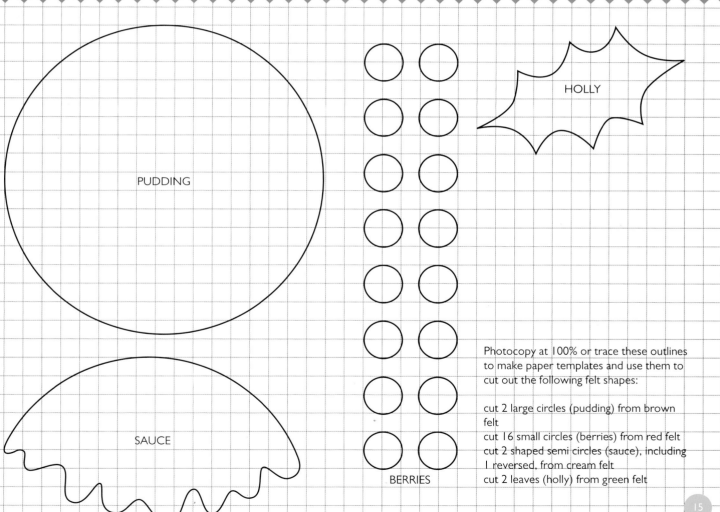

PUDDING

SAUCE

HOLLY

BERRIES

Photocopy at 100% or trace these outlines to make paper templates and use them to cut out the following felt shapes:

cut 2 large circles (pudding) from brown felt
cut 16 small circles (berries) from red felt
cut 2 shaped semi circles (sauce), including 1 reversed, from cream felt
cut 2 leaves (holly) from green felt

15

How to Make the Christmas Pudding

1 Assemble all the materials, equipment and templates you need, as listed on page 15.

2 Following the guides on pages 8–9, and using an air-erasable pen, trace the outline of each paper template onto the correct colour felt.

3 Following the outlines carefully, cut out all the felt shapes you need, as listed on page 15.

4 Place the cream shaped semi circles over the brown circles and work small edging stitches along the bottom edge with cream thread.

5 Place 8 small red circles over each of the visible brown circles and work small edging stitches all the way round in red thread.

6 Along the length of each green holly leaf, work a line of running stitch from down the centre in brown thread.

7 Stitch both holly leaves to the top of one side of the pudding, with tips overlapping. Add the red pompoms where the holly leaves meet.

8 Place both sides of the pudding together and work edging stitches all the way round in brown and cream thread, leaving a gap at the top.

9 Fill the pudding with toy stuffing, but do not overfill. Use the rounded end of a pencil to push the stuffing gently into any curves or corners.

10 Stitch the gap to enclose the stuffing, adding the hanging loop of waxed cord. Knot the cord ends and work extra stitches over it to secure.

Holly & Berries

You will need

From the gift pack: Green felt • Brown embroidery thread • Two red pompoms
• 15cm brown waxed cord for hanging loop

You will also need: Paper templates • Air-erasable pen • Sewing needle • Scissors
• Polyester toy stuffing (see safety note on page 64)

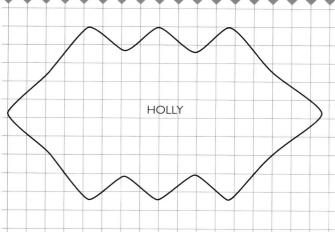

HOLLY

Photocopy at 100% or trace this outline to make paper templates
and use them to cut out the following felt shapes:

cut 4 large leaves (holly), including 2 reversed, from green felt

How to Make the Holly & Berries

1 Assemble all the materials, equipment and templates you need, as listed on page 19.

2 Following the guides on pages 8–9, and using an air-erasable pen, trace the outline of each paper template onto the correct colour felt.

3 Following the outlines carefully, cut out all the felt shapes you need, as listed on page 19.

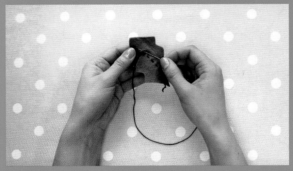

4 Along the length of each holly leaf, work a line of running stitch down the centre in brown thread. Work more lines out from the centre.

5 Place both sides of each holly leaf together and work edging stitches all the way round in brown thread, leaving a gap at the top.

6 Fill each holly leaf with toy stuffing, but do not overfill. Use the rounded end of a pencil to push the stuffing gently into any curves or corners.

7 Stitch the gaps to enclose the stuffing, adding the hanging loop of waxed cord to one leaf. Work extra stitches over the cord to secure.

8 With their tips overlapping, join the holly leaves together with a few extra stitches. Add the red pompoms where the holly leaves meet.

Gift-Wrapped Present

You will need

From the gift pack: Red, green, pink, blue and cream felt • Red, cream and brown embroidery thread • 15cm length brown waxed cord

You will also need: Paper templates • Air-erasable pen • Sewing needle • Scissors • Polyester toy stuffing (see safety note on page 64)

PRESENT

RIBBON

FLOWER

GIFT TAG

Photocopy at 100% or trace these outlines to make paper templates and use them to cut out the following felt shapes:

cut 2 large squares (present) from red felt
cut 4 rectangles (ribbon) from green felt
cut 4 flowers from pink felt
cut 4 flowers from blue felt
cut 4 flowers from cream felt
cut 1 small rectangle (gift tag) from cream felt

How to Make the Gift-Wrapped Present

1 Assemble all the materials, equipment and templates you need, as listed on page 23.

2 Following the guides on pages 8–9, and using an air-erasable pen, trace the outline of each paper template onto the correct colour felt.

3 Following the outlines carefully, cut out all the felt shapes you need, as listed on page 23.

4 Place 4 small flowers randomly over each of the red squares and work small edging stitches all the way round in cream thread.

5 Place 2 more flowers in the corners of the red squares and work edging stitches part the way round. Trim away any excess felt.

6 Embroider a French knot in the centre of each flower in red thread.

7 Place a green rectangle vertically over the red squares and work edging stitches along both sides in cream thread.

8 Place another green rectangle horizontally over the red squares, one third of the way down from the top, and work edging stitches along both sides in cream thread.

9 Place both sides of the present together and work edging stitches all the way round in red thread, leaving a small gap at the top.

10 Fill the present with toy stuffing, but do not overfill. Use the rounded end of a pencil to push the stuffing gently into any curves or corners.

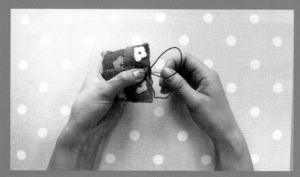

11 Stitch the gap to enclose the stuffing, adding the hanging loop of waxed cord. Knot the cord ends and work extra stitches over it to secure.

12 Embroider the small cream rectangle with your chosen initials and stitch to one side of the present where the green ribbons overlap.

Winter Reindeer

You will need

From the gift pack: Red, brown, cream and pink felt • Red, brown and cream embroidery thread • 15cm length brown waxed cord

You will also need: Paper templates • Air-erasable pen • Sewing needle • Scissors • Polyester toy stuffing (see safety note on page 64)

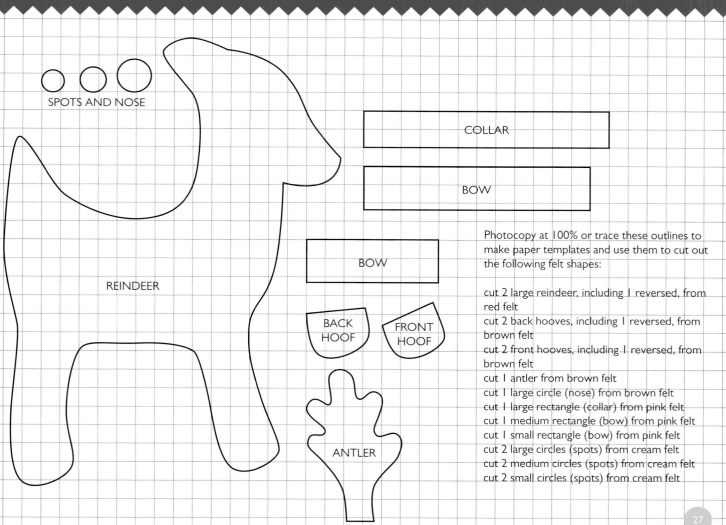

SPOTS AND NOSE

COLLAR

BOW

REINDEER

BOW

BACK HOOF

FRONT HOOF

ANTLER

Photocopy at 100% or trace these outlines to make paper templates and use them to cut out the following felt shapes:

cut 2 large reindeer, including 1 reversed, from red felt
cut 2 back hooves, including 1 reversed, from brown felt
cut 2 front hooves, including 1 reversed, from brown felt
cut 1 antler from brown felt
cut 1 large circle (nose) from brown felt
cut 1 large rectangle (collar) from pink felt
cut 1 medium rectangle (bow) from pink felt
cut 1 small rectangle (bow) from pink felt
cut 2 large circles (spots) from cream felt
cut 2 medium circles (spots) from cream felt
cut 2 small circles (spots) from cream felt

27

How to Make the Reindeer

1 Assemble all the materials, equipment and templates you need, as listed on page 27.

2 Following the guides on pages 8–9, and using an air-erasable pen, trace the outline of each paper template onto the correct colour felt.

3 Following the outlines carefully, cut out all the felt shapes you need, as listed on page 27.

4 Embroider a French knot on the head of each reindeer, in the correct position for the eyes, in brown thread.

5 Place a cream circle in each size over the rump of both reindeer and work small edging stitches all the way round in cream thread.

6 Place the brown back and front hooves over the feet of both reindeer and work small edging stitches all the way round in brown thread.

7 Place both sides of the reindeer together, with the antlers and nose in between. Work stitches all the way round, leaving a gap in the back.

8 Fill the reindeer with toy stuffing, but do not overfill. Use the rounded end of a pencil to push the stuffing gently into any curves or corners.

9 Stitch the gap to enclose the stuffing, adding the hanging loop of waxed cord. Knot the cord ends and work extra stitches over it to secure.

10 Wrap the short pink strip around the folded medium strip to make a bow. Stitch the longer pink strip around the neck and attach the bow.

Santa Claus

You will need

From the gift pack: Red, cream and pink felt • Red, brown and cream embroidery thread
• One white pompom • 15cm length brown waxed cord

You will also need: Paper templates • Air-erasable pen • Sewing needle • Scissors
• Polyester toy stuffing (see safety note on page 64)

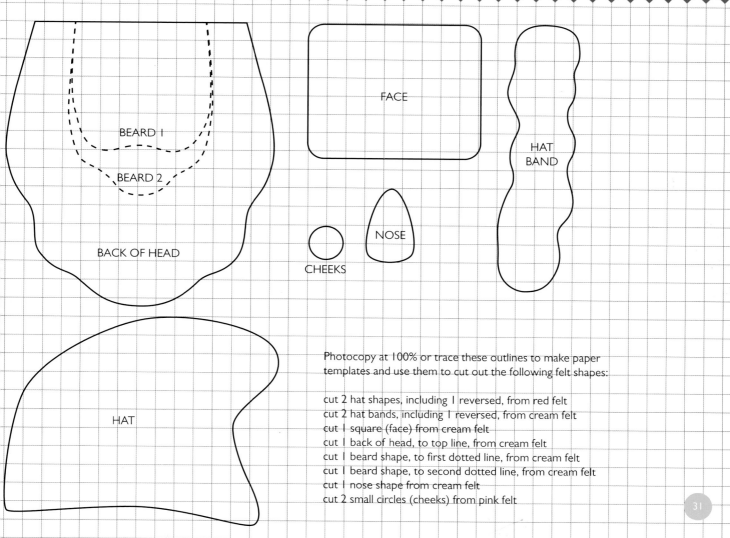

BEARD 1

BEARD 2

BACK OF HEAD

FACE

HAT BAND

NOSE

CHEEKS

HAT

Photocopy at 100% or trace these outlines to make paper templates and use them to cut out the following felt shapes:

cut 2 hat shapes, including 1 reversed, from red felt
cut 2 hat bands, including 1 reversed, from cream felt
cut 1 square (face) from cream felt
cut 1 back of head, to top line, from cream felt
cut 1 beard shape, to first dotted line, from cream felt
cut 1 beard shape, to second dotted line, from cream felt
cut 1 nose shape from cream felt
cut 2 small circles (cheeks) from pink felt

How to Make the Santa Claus

1 Assemble all the materials, equipment and templates you need, as listed on page 31.

2 Following the guides on pages 8–9, and using an air-erasable pen, trace the outline of each paper template onto the correct colour felt.

3 Following the outlines carefully, cut out all the felt shapes you need, as listed on page 31. Pay particular attention to any shapes that must be reversed or dotted lines followed.

4 Place the largest cream beard over the square cream face and work small edging stitches all round the inside edge in cream thread. Add the nose and cheeks.

5 Lay the second cream beard over the face and first beard and stitch in place at the top side edges only, so the beard flaps freely.

6 Embroider French knots above the nose, in the correct positions for the eyes, in brown thread. Work a line of backstitch in red thread for the mouth.

7 Place the cream hat bands over the red hats and work small edging stitches along the inside edges in cream thread.

8 Place the red hats, with bands attached, over the top of the front and back heads to match and work edging stitches in cream thread.

9 Place the front and back heads together and work edging stitches all the way round in red and cream thread, leaving a small gap at the top.

10 Fill the Santa with toy stuffing, but do not overfill. Use the rounded end of a pencil to push the stuffing gently into any curves or corners.

11 Stitch the gap to enclose the stuffing, adding the hanging loop of waxed cord. Knot the cord ends and work extra stitches over it to secure.

12 Add the white pompom to the tip of the hat, working a few small stitches to secure.

Frosty Snowman

You will need

From the gift pack: Red, brown, cream and green felt • Red, brown and cream embroidery thread • 15cm length brown waxed cord

You will also need: Paper templates • Air-erasable pen • Sewing needle • Scissors • Polyester toy stuffing (see safety note on page 64)

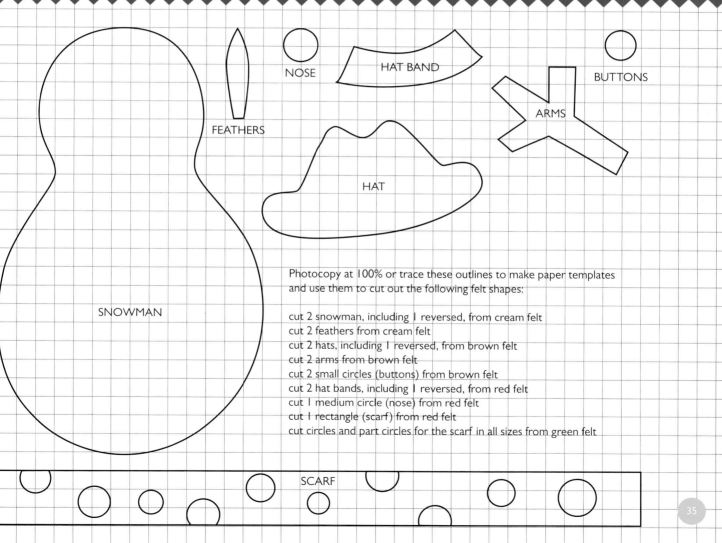

NOSE

HAT BAND

BUTTONS

ARMS

FEATHERS

HAT

SNOWMAN

Photocopy at 100% or trace these outlines to make paper templates and use them to cut out the following felt shapes:

cut 2 snowman, including 1 reversed, from cream felt
cut 2 feathers from cream felt
cut 2 hats, including 1 reversed, from brown felt
cut 2 arms from brown felt
cut 2 small circles (buttons) from brown felt
cut 2 hat bands, including 1 reversed, from red felt
cut 1 medium circle (nose) from red felt
cut 1 rectangle (scarf) from red felt
cut circles and part circles for the scarf in all sizes from green felt

SCARF

How to Make the Frosty Snowman

1 Assemble all the materials, equipment and templates you need, as listed on page 35.

2 Following the guides on pages 8–9, and using an air-erasable pen, trace the outline of each paper template onto the correct colour felt.

3 Following the outlines carefully, cut out all the felt shapes you need, as listed on page 35.

4 Embroider French knots on a snowman, in the correct positions for the eyes, in brown thread. Add the nose and buttons and stitch in place.

5 Place the red hat bands over the brown hats and work small edging stitches along the edges in red thread.

6 Place the brown hats over the top of the front and back heads of the snowman to match and work edging stitches in brown thread.

7 Make snips in both sides of the feathers. Along the length of each feather, work a line of running stitch down the centre in brown thread.

8 Stitch both feathers to the front hat band, slightly off to one side, with the tips overlapping. Secure with a few extra stitches.

9 Place both sides of the snowman together, with the arms in between. Work edging stitches all the way round in cream and brown thread, leaving a small gap at the top.

10 Fill the snowman with toy stuffing, but do not overfill. Use the rounded end of a pencil to push the stuffing gently into any curves or corners.

11 Stitch the gap to enclose the stuffing, adding the hanging loop of waxed cord. Knot the cord ends and work extra stitches over it to secure.

12 Place the green circles and part circles over the red scarf and stitch in place. Wrap around the snowman's neck, crossing the ends, and secure with a few stitches.

Christmas Angel

You will need

From the gift pack: Red, brown, cream, green, pink and blue felt • Red, brown and cream embroidery thread • 15cm length brown waxed cord

You will also need: Paper templates • Air-erasable pen • Sewing needle • Scissors • Polyester toy stuffing (see safety note on page 64)

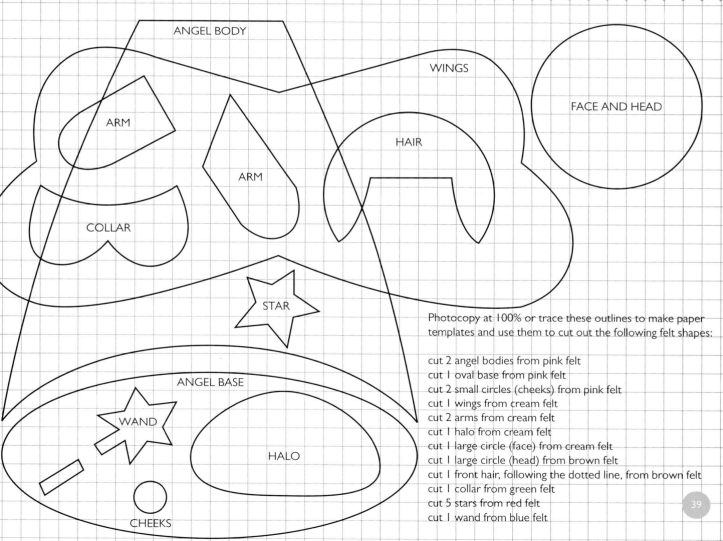

ANGEL BODY

WINGS

FACE AND HEAD

ARM

ARM

HAIR

COLLAR

STAR

ANGEL BASE

WAND

HALO

CHEEKS

Photocopy at 100% or trace these outlines to make paper templates and use them to cut out the following felt shapes:

cut 2 angel bodies from pink felt
cut 1 oval base from pink felt
cut 2 small circles (cheeks) from pink felt
cut 1 wings from cream felt
cut 2 arms from cream felt
cut 1 halo from cream felt
cut 1 large circle (face) from cream felt
cut 1 large circle (head) from brown felt
cut 1 front hair, following the dotted line, from brown felt
cut 1 collar from green felt
cut 5 stars from red felt
cut 1 wand from blue felt

39

How to Make the Christmas Angel

1 Assemble all the materials, equipment and templates you need, as listed on page 39.

2 Following the guides on pages 8–9, and using an air-erasable pen, trace the outline of each paper template onto the correct colour felt.

3 Following the outlines carefully, cut out all the felt shapes you need, as listed on page 39.

4 Place the front hair over the face and work edging stitches in brown thread. Add the pink cheeks, overlapping the hair. Embroider French knots for eyes in brown thread.

5 Place the bodies over the front and back heads to match and join with edging stitches in cream thread. Add red stars over the bodies and stitch in place with red thread.

6 Place the arms over the front body, tucking the blue wand underneath the longer right arm, and work small edging stitches all the way round in cream thread.

7 Place the green collar over the front neck and stitch all the way round. Slide the cream halo onto the top of the brown hair and stitch along the edges.

8 Place the wings over the back body, aligning the centres, and work a line of running stitch or backstitch down the centre in cream thread.

9 Place both sides of the angel together and work edging stitches all the way up each side in cream thread, leaving a gap at the top of the head.

10 Place the oval base at the bottom edge of the body, carefully aligning the edges, and work small edging stitches all the way round in cream thread.

11 Fill the angel with toy stuffing, but do not overfill. Use the rounded end of a pencil to push the stuffing gently into any curves or corners.

12 Stitch the gap to enclose the stuffing, adding the hanging loop of waxed cord. Knot the cord ends and work extra stitches over it to secure.

Striped Stocking

You will need

From the gift pack: Red, cream and green felt • Red and cream embroidery thread
• Two red pompoms • 15cm length brown waxed cord

You will also need: Paper templates • Air-erasable pen • Sewing needle • Scissors
• Polyester toy stuffing (see safety note on page 64)

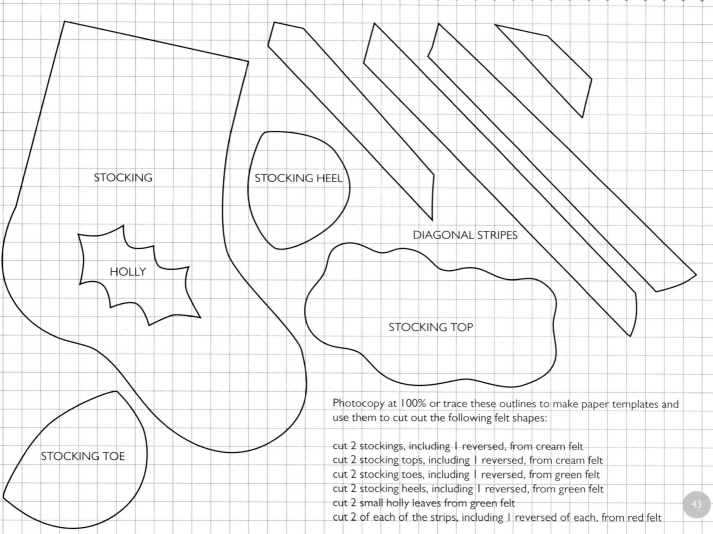

STOCKING

STOCKING HEEL

DIAGONAL STRIPES

HOLLY

STOCKING TOP

STOCKING TOE

Photocopy at 100% or trace these outlines to make paper templates and
use them to cut out the following felt shapes:

cut 2 stockings, including 1 reversed, from cream felt
cut 2 stocking tops, including 1 reversed, from cream felt
cut 2 stocking toes, including 1 reversed, from green felt
cut 2 stocking heels, including 1 reversed, from green felt
cut 2 small holly leaves from green felt
cut 2 of each of the strips, including 1 reversed of each, from red felt

How to Make the Striped Stocking

1 Assemble all the materials, equipment and templates you need, as listed on page 43.

2 Following the guides on pages 8–9, and using an air-erasable pen, trace the outline of each paper template onto the correct colour felt.

3 Following the outlines carefully, cut out all the felt shapes you need, as listed on page 43. Pay particular attention to any shapes that must be reversed.

4 Place the red stripes, in the correct order, over the cream stockings and work small edging stitches along each edge in red thread.

5 Place the cream stocking tops over the top of the striped stockings to match and work small edging stitches along the lower edges in cream thread.

6 Place the green heels and toes over the foot of the striped stockings and work small edging stitches along the inside edge in cream thread.

7 Place both sides of the stocking together and work small edging stitches all the way round in cream or red thread, leaving a gap at the top.

8 Fill the stocking with toy stuffing, but do not overfill. Use the rounded end of a pencil to push the stuffing gently into any curves or corners.

9 Stitch the gap to enclose the stuffing, adding the hanging loop of waxed cord. Knot the cord ends and work extra stitches over it to secure.

10 Prepare the holly leaves, then add them to the top of the stocking with the red pompoms, following the instructions on pages 14–15.

Snowy Cottage

You will need

From the gift pack: Red, brown, cream, green, pink and blue felt • Red, brown and cream embroidery thread • 15cm length brown waxed cord

You will also need: Paper templates • Air-erasable pen • Sewing needle • Scissors
• Polyester toy stuffing (see safety note on page 64)

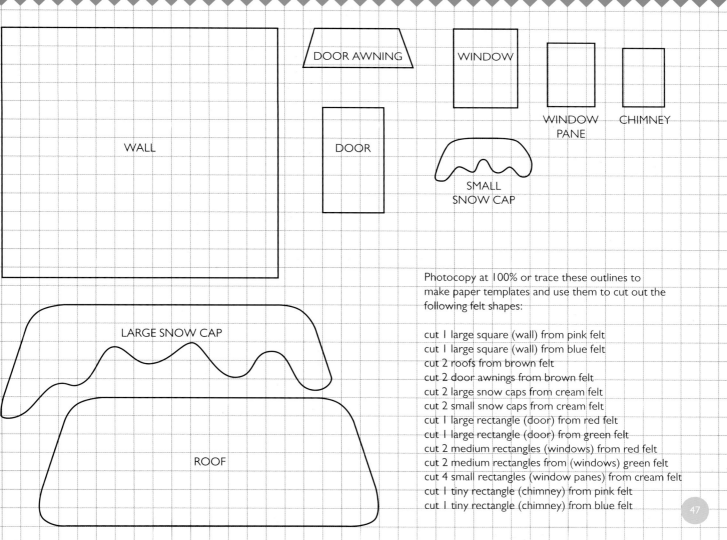

WALL

DOOR AWNING

DOOR

WINDOW

WINDOW PANE

CHIMNEY

SMALL SNOW CAP

LARGE SNOW CAP

ROOF

Photocopy at 100% or trace these outlines to make paper templates and use them to cut out the following felt shapes:

cut 1 large square (wall) from pink felt
cut 1 large square (wall) from blue felt
cut 2 roofs from brown felt
cut 2 door awnings from brown felt
cut 2 large snow caps from cream felt
cut 2 small snow caps from cream felt
cut 1 large rectangle (door) from red felt
cut 1 large rectangle (door) from green felt
cut 2 medium rectangles (windows) from red felt
cut 2 medium rectangles from (windows) green felt
cut 4 small rectangles (window panes) from cream felt
cut 1 tiny rectangle (chimney) from pink felt
cut 1 tiny rectangle (chimney) from blue felt

How to Make the Snowy Cottage

1 Assemble all the materials, equipment and templates you need, as listed on page 47.

2 Following the guides on pages 8–9, and using an air-erasable pen, trace the outline of each paper template onto the correct colour felt.

3 Following the outlines carefully, cut out all the felt shapes you need, as listed on page 47. Pay particular attention to any shapes that must be reversed.

4 Place the red door over the pink walls. Place the green door over the blue walls. Stitch in place with red or cream thread. Add the brown awnings and cream small snow caps.

5 Place the red and green windows either side of the door on the respective pink and blue walls. Stitch in place.

6 Embroider French knots on the doors, in the correct position for the handles, in brown thread.

7 Place the cream window panes over the windows and work long straight stitches vertically and horizontally in brown thread for the window bars.

8 Place the cream large snow caps over the brown roofs and stitch in place. Place the snowy roofs over the pink and blue walls and stitch in place.

9 Place both sides of the cottage together and work edging stitches all the way round in cream thread, leaving a small gap at the top.

10 Fill the cottage with toy stuffing, but do not overfill. Use the rounded end of a pencil to push the stuffing gently into any curves and corners.

11 Stitch the gap to enclose the stuffing, adding the hanging loop of waxed cord. Knot the cord ends and work extra stitches over it to secure.

10 Place the pink and blue chimneys either side at one end of the roof, sandwiching a tiny piece of toy stuffing in between. Stitch to secure.

Christmas Robin

You will need

From the gift pack: Red, brown, cream and green felt • Red, brown and cream embroidery thread • One white pompom • 15cm length brown waxed cord

You will also need: Paper templates • Air-erasable pen • Sewing needle • Scissors • Polyester toy stuffing (see safety note on page 64)

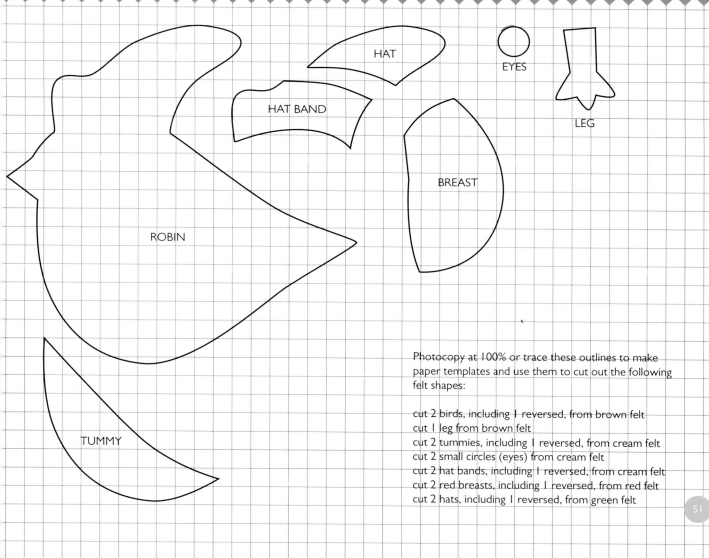

HAT

EYES

HAT BAND

LEG

BREAST

ROBIN

TUMMY

Photocopy at 100% or trace these outlines to make paper templates and use them to cut out the following felt shapes:

cut 2 birds, including 1 reversed, from brown felt
cut 1 leg from brown felt
cut 2 tummies, including 1 reversed, from cream felt
cut 2 small circles (eyes) from cream felt
cut 2 hat bands, including 1 reversed, from cream felt
cut 2 red breasts, including 1 reversed, from red felt
cut 2 hats, including 1 reversed, from green felt

How to Make the Christmas Robin

1 Assemble all the materials, equipment and templates you need, as listed on page 51.

2 Following the guides on pages 8–9, and using an air-erasable pen, trace the outline of each paper template onto the correct colour felt.

3 Following the outlines carefully, cut out all the felt shapes you need, as listed on page 51. Pay particular attention to any shapes that must be reversed.

4 Place the cream tummies over the brown bodies and work small edging stitches along the inside edges in cream thread.

5 Place the red breasts over the brown bodies, overlapping the cream tummies, and work edging stitches along the inside edges in red thread.

6 Place the cream eyes over the red breasts. Stitch in place with cream thread. Embroider French knots on the cream eyes in brown thread.

7 Place the cream hat bands over the green hats and work small edging stitches along the inside edge in cream thread.

8 Place the green hats, with bands attached, over the top of the heads to match and work edging stitches along the lower edges in cream thread.

9 Place both sides of the robin together with the legs in between. Work edging stitches all the way round in brown thread, leaving a small gap at the top.

10 Fill the robin with toy stuffing, but do not overfill. Use the rounded end of a pencil to push the stuffing into any curves or corners.

11 Stitch the gap to enclose the stuffing, adding the hanging loop of waxed cord. Knot the cord ends and work extra stitches over it to secure.

12 Add the white pompom to the tip of the hat, working a few small stitches to secure.

Christmas Tree

You will need

From the gift pack: Red, brown, cream, green, pink and blue felt • Red, brown and cream embroidery thread • 15cm length brown waxed cord

You will also need: Paper templates • Air-erasable pen • Sewing needle • Scissors • Polyester toy stuffing (see safety note on page 64)

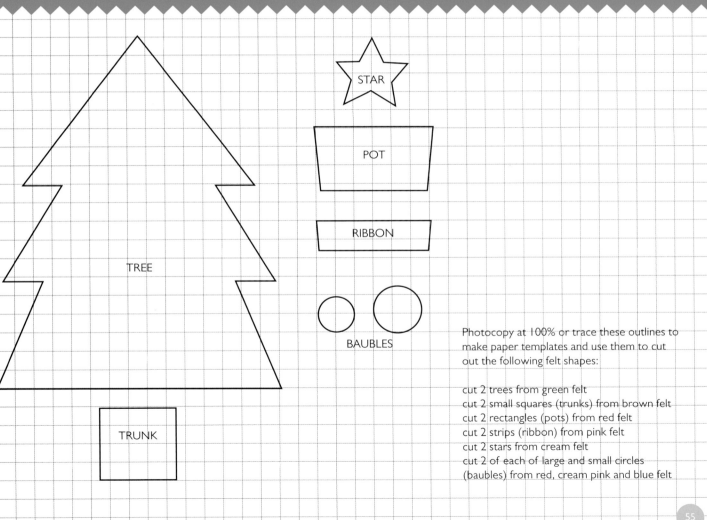

STAR

POT

RIBBON

TREE

BAUBLES

TRUNK

Photocopy at 100% or trace these outlines to make paper templates and use them to cut out the following felt shapes:

cut 2 trees from green felt
cut 2 small squares (trunks) from brown felt
cut 2 rectangles (pots) from red felt
cut 2 strips (ribbon) from pink felt
cut 2 stars from cream felt
cut 2 of each of large and small circles (baubles) from red, cream pink and blue felt

How to Make the Christmas Tree

1 Assemble all the materials, equipment and templates you need, as listed on page 55.

2 Following the guides on pages 8–9, and using an air-erasable pen, trace the outline of each paper template onto the correct colour felt.

3 Following the outlines carefully, cut out all the felt shapes you need, as listed on page 55.

4 Work criss-crossing diagonal lines of running stitch across both green trees, taking the lines from edge to edge, in cream thread.

5 Place the different size circles over the green trees, placing two of each colour on each piece, and work small edging stitches all the way round.

6 Place the red pots over the brown trunks and work small edging stitches along the adjoining edges in red thread.

7 Place the pink strips over the red pots and work small edging stitches along the edges in red thread.

8 Place the green trees over the brown trunks and work edging stitches along the adjoining edges in brown thread.

9 Place both sides of the tree together and work edging stitches all the way round the outside, leaving a small gap at the top.

10 Fill the tree with toy stuffing, but do not overfill. Use the rounded end of a pencil to push the stuffing gently into any curves or corners.

11 Stitch the gap to enclose the stuffing, adding the hanging loop of waxed cord. Knot the cord ends and work extra stitches over it to secure.

12 Add the cream stars to the top of the tree, placing one on either side of the hanging cord, and working edging stitches all the way round.

Festive Stanley

You will need

From the gift pack: Red, brown, cream, green, pink and blue felt • Red, brown and cream embroidery thread • 15cm length brown waxed cord

You will also need: Paper templates • Air-erasable pen • Sewing needle • Scissors • Polyester toy stuffing (see safety note on page 64)

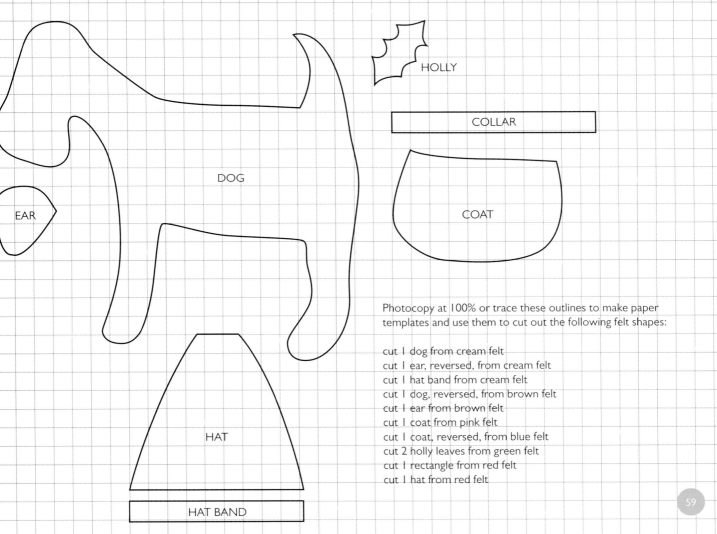

HOLLY

COLLAR

DOG

EAR

COAT

HAT

HAT BAND

Photocopy at 100% or trace these outlines to make paper templates and use them to cut out the following felt shapes:

cut 1 dog from cream felt
cut 1 ear, reversed, from cream felt
cut 1 hat band from cream felt
cut 1 dog, reversed, from brown felt
cut 1 ear from brown felt
cut 1 coat from pink felt
cut 1 coat, reversed, from blue felt
cut 2 holly leaves from green felt
cut 1 rectangle from red felt
cut 1 hat from red felt

59

How to Make the Festive Stanley

1 Assemble all the materials, equipment and templates you need, as listed on page 59.

2 Following the guides on pages 8–9, and using an air-erasable pen, trace the outline of each paper template onto the correct colour felt.

3 Following the outlines carefully, cut out all the felt shapes you need, as listed on page 59. Pay particular attention to any shapes that must be reversed.

4 Place the brown ear over the cream dog. Place the cream ear over the brown dog. Stitch in place with cream and brown thread.

4 Place the pink coat over the cream dog. Place the blue coat over the brown dog. Stitch in place with cream and brown thread.

5 Embroider French knots, in the correct positions for the eyes, in brown thread on the cream dog and in cream thread on the brown dog.

6 Place the dogs together and work edging stitches all the way round, leaving a small gap at the centre back.

Fill the dog with toy stuffing, but do not overfill. Use the rounded end of a pencil to push the stuffing gently into any curves or corners.

8 Stitch the gap to enclose the stuffing, adding the hanging loop of waxed cord. Knot the cord ends and work extra stitches over it to secure.

9 Lay the cream hat band over the red hat and stitch in place with cream thread. Fold the red hat in half and join along the side seam with red thread.

10 Place the hat, with band attached, on the top of the dog's head and stitch in place. Embroider a small nose on the front central seam with a few long straight stitches.

11 Wrap the red strip around Stanley's neck and join the ends to make the collar. Add the holly leaves and red pompoms to the collar.

Cath Kidston Stores

Aberdeen
Unit GS20
Union Square Shopping Centre
Aberdeen AB11 5PN
01224 591 726

Bath
3 Broad Street
Milsom Place
Bath BA1 5LJ
01225 331 006

Belfast
24–26 Arthur Street
Belfast BT1 4GF
02890 231 581

Bluewater
Unit L003 Rose Gallery
Bluewater Centre DA9 9SH
01322 387 454

Bournemouth
5–6 The Arcade
Old Christchurch Road
Bournemouth BH1 2AF
01202 553 848

Brighton
31a & 32 East Street
Brighton BN1 1HL
01273 227 420

Bristol
79 Park Street
Bristol BS1 5PF
0117 930 4722

Cambridge
31–33 Market Hill
Cambridge CB2 3NU
01223 351 810

Canterbury
6 The Parade
Canterbury CT1 2JL
01227 455 639

Cardiff
45 The Hayes
St David's
Cardiff CF10 1GA
02920 225 627

Cheltenham
21 The Promenade
Cheltenham GL50 1LE
01242 245 912

Chester
12 Eastgate Streets
Chester CH1 1LE
01244 310 685

Chichester
24 South Street
Chichester PO19 1EL
01243 850 100

Dublin
Unit CSD 1.3
Dundrum Shopping Centre
Dublin 16
01 296 4430

Edinburgh
58 George Street
Edinburgh EH2 2LR
0131 220 1509

Exeter
6 Princesshay
Exeter EX1 1GE
01392 227 835

Glasgow
18 Gordon Street
Glasgow G1 3PB
0141 248 2773

Guildford
14–18 Chertsey Street
Guildford GU1 4HD
01483 564 798

Harrogate
2–6 James Street
Harrogate HG1 1RF
01423 531 481

Jersey
11 King Street
St Helier JE2 4WF
01534 726 768

Kildare
Unit 21c Kildare Village
Nurney Road
Kildare Town
00 353 45 535 084

Kingston
10 Thames Street
Kingston Upon Thames KT1 1PE
020 8546 6760

Leeds
26 Lands Lane
Leeds LS1 6LB
0113 391 2692

Liverpool
18 School Lane
Liverpool L1 3BT
0151 709 2747

London – Battersea
142 Northcote Road
London SW11 6RD
020 7228 6571

London – Chiswick
125 Chiswick High Road
London W4 2ED
020 8995 8052

London – Covent Garden
28–32 Shelton Street
London WC2H 9JE
020 7836 4803

London – Fulham
668 Fulham Road
London SW6 5RX
020 7731 6531

London – Heathrow Terminal 4
Heathrow Airport TW6 3XA
020 8759 5578

London – Kings Road
322 Kings Road
London SW3 5UH
020 7351 7335

London – Marylebone
51 Marylebone High Street
London W1U 5HW
020 7935 6555

London – Notting Hill
158 Portobello Road
London W11 2BE
020 7727 0043

London – Sloane Square
27 Kings Road
London SW3 4RP
020 7259 9847

London – St Pancras
St Pancras International Station
London NW1 2QP
020 7837 4125

London – Wimbledon Village
3 High Street
Wimbledon SW19 5DX
020 8944 1001

Manchester
62 King Street
Manchester M2 4ND
0161 8347 936

Marlborough
142–142a High Street
Marlborough SN8 1HN
01672 512 514

Marlow
6 Market Square
Marlow SL7 1DA
01628 484 443

Newbury
Unit G42 Middle Street
Parkway
Newbury RG14 1AY

Newcastle
136–138 Grainger Street
Newcastle NE1 5AF

Norwich
21 Castle Street
Norwich NR2 1PB

Nottingham
23 Bridesmith Gate
Nottingham NG1 2GR

Oxford
6 Broad Street
Oxford OX1 3AJ
01865 791 576

Reading
96 Broad Street
Reading RG1 2AP
01189 588 530

St Albans
Unit 4 Christopher Place
St Albans AL3 5DQ
01727 810 432

St Ives
67 Fore Street
St Ives TR26 1HE
01736 798 001

Sheffield
60 High Street
Meadowhall
Sheffield S9 1EN

Tunbridge Wells
59–61 High Street
Tunbridge Wells TN1 1XU
01892 521 197

Winchester
46 High Street
Winchester SO23 9BT
01962 870 620

Windsor
24 High Street
Windsor SL4 1LH
01753 830 591

York
32 Stonegate
York YO1 8AS
01904 733 653

Concessions in:
Bicester Village, OX26 6WD
Gunwharf Quays, PO1 3TU
Fenwicks, Northumberland Street,
Newcastle Upon Tyne NE99 1AR
Selfridges, The Bull Ring,
Birmingham B5 4BP
Selfridges, Oxford Street,
London W1A 1AB
Selfridges, Exchange Square,
Manchester M3 1BD
Selfridges, Trafford Centre,
Manchester M17 8DA

**For up-to-date
information on all
Cath Kidston stores,
please visit
www.cathkidston.com**

Acknowledgements

My special thanks to everyone involved in the creation of this book: to Jessica Pemberton for the making of the projects, Elaine Ashton, Jamie Royden and Nina Suwala. To Claire Richardson and Lara Hall for the photography, and to Anne Furniss, Helen Lewis, Lisa Pendreigh and Katherine Case at Quadrille Publishing.

Cath Kidston

Series Creative Coordinator
Elaine Ashton
Design Assistant to Cath Kidston
Jessica Pemberton
Stylist Lara Hall
Production coordinators
Jamie Royden and Nina Suwala

Editorial Director Anne Furniss
Creative Director Helen Lewis
Project Editor Lisa Pendreigh
Designer Katherine Case
Photographer Claire Richardson
Sewing Assistant Gemma Hogan
Hand Model Chinh Hoang
Production Director Vincent Smith
Production Controller Aysun Hughes

If you have any comments or queries regarding the instructions in this book, please contact us at enquiries@quadrille.co.uk.

First published in 2012 by Quadrille Publishing Limited
Alhambra House, 27–31 Charing Cross Road, London WC2H 0LS

Project design and templates © Cath Kidston 2012
Photography © Claire Richardson 2012
Text, illustration, design and layout copyright © Quadrille Publishing Limited 2012

Cataloguing-in-Publication Data: a catalogue record for this book is available from the British Library.

ISBN 978 1 84949 182 2

SAFETY NOTES
These Christmas decorations are not designed to be used as toys, so therefore are unsuitable for children under the age of 3 years. Small children should only make these decorations under adult supervision due to the necessary use of sharp scissors and sewing needles.
Always use a polyester toy stuffing that is non-flammable (flame retardant), non-toxic and adheres to UK and EU safety regulations (BS1425, BS5852, EN71, PT2).